Tom Woo

Progressive Scale and Arpeggio Studies

for Trumpet

2nd Edition

Printed in the United States of America

First Printing, 2016

ISBN 978-1-7360876-1-9

Center Stage Publishing
P.O. Box 622
Mountain View, CA 94042

www.takecenterstage.today

Contents

Who Should Use This Book

This book is best for teenage and adult musicians at the beginner or intermediate levels, younger players that are learning with a teacher, parent or older sibling, and adults who are returning to music after a long time off. More advanced musicians could also use it for reviewing and refining scale and arpeggio patterns, since it never hurts to keep expanding your range, volume, and speed.

Why Scales and Arpeggios?

For many of us, our enjoyment of playing an instrument comes largely from how well it lets us freely share something about ourselves. As a musician, one of your primary ambitions may be reaching a point where all you have to think about is what you want to say with your music. You might even feel that any thoughts about mechanics or technique (which valves to press, how tight your lips should be for an upcoming note, etc.) are a distraction and limit your self-expression.

Part of removing these mechanical distractions is having the "muscle memory" of many musical patterns, so that you really do not have to think about them. Practicing scales and arpeggios have long been a great way to accomplish this, and this book was written to support you by organizing many scales and arpeggios into one place for you to progress through systematically.

How To Use This Book

You should use this book as a supplement to any typical course of trumpet learning, such as one that might include a private instructor and method books by J.-B. Arban, Max Schlossberg, Herbert L. Clarke, Walter M. Smith, James Stamp, and others. I've intentionally left out tempo and articulation markings, with the idea that a student would keep the following suggestions in mind:

- For each exercise, start with a tempo that lets you to play with accurate pitches and rhythms while keeping the tempo steady. Then, gradually increase the tempo from there.
- Play the exercises in various styles and volumes and with various articulations, including completely slurred.
- Play the exercises in octaves other than the ones written.
- Don't avoid the exercises written in (seemingly) "difficult" keys. Try to see it this way: there are no bad notes on the trumpet or bad key signatures for trumpet music, only notes and key signatures that *you* might not have mastered. Working through these could remove many of the limitations to your artistic expression.

 If you're a beginner or a less experienced player, you might find the tips and suggestions marked with this icon to be useful.

Most of this book is only the beginning of a trumpet player's journey. I hope that it gives you some part of a solid foundation that enables you to approach all the great musical opportunities in the world with confidence.

Have fun!

Part 1 - Getting Started

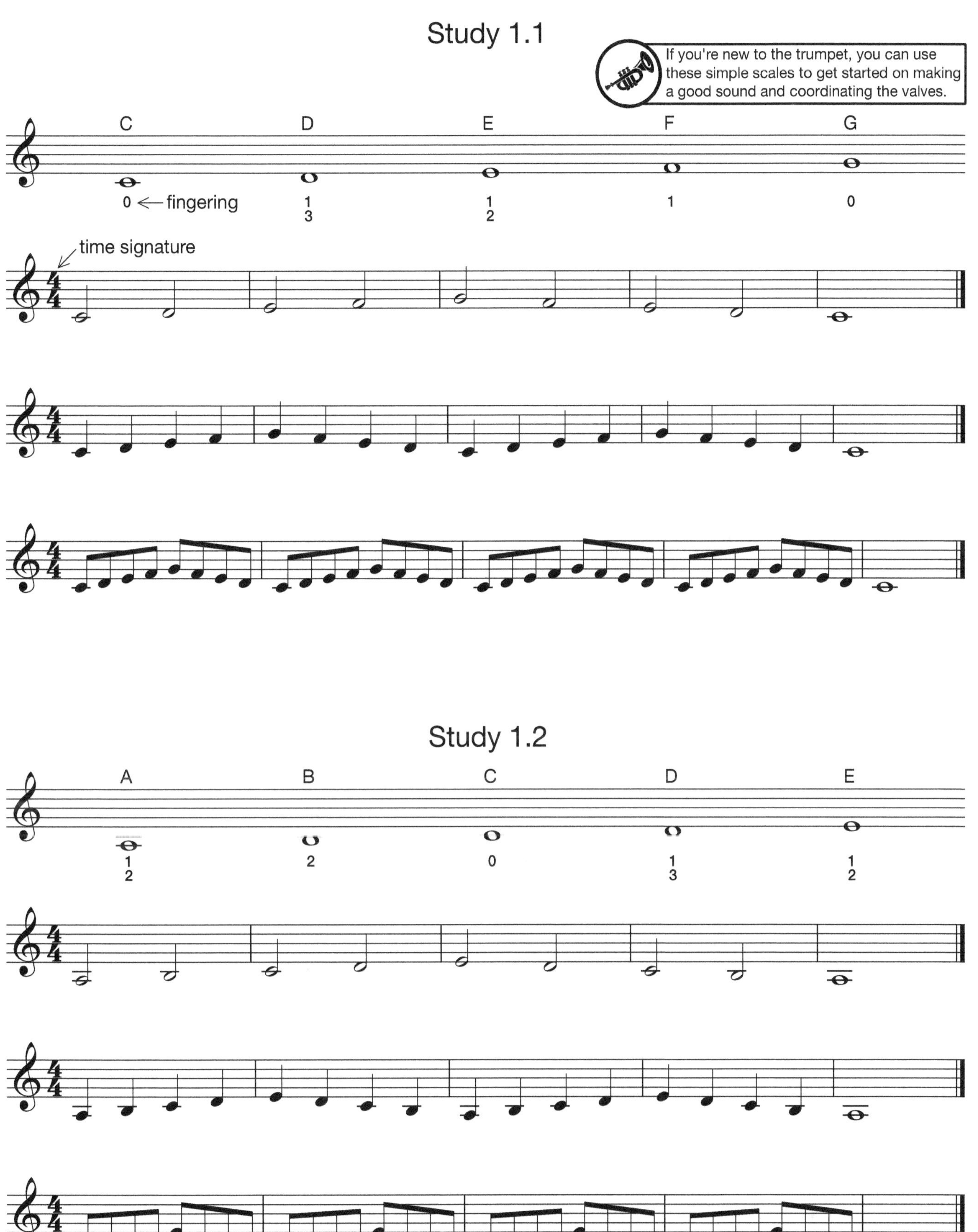

Study 1.3

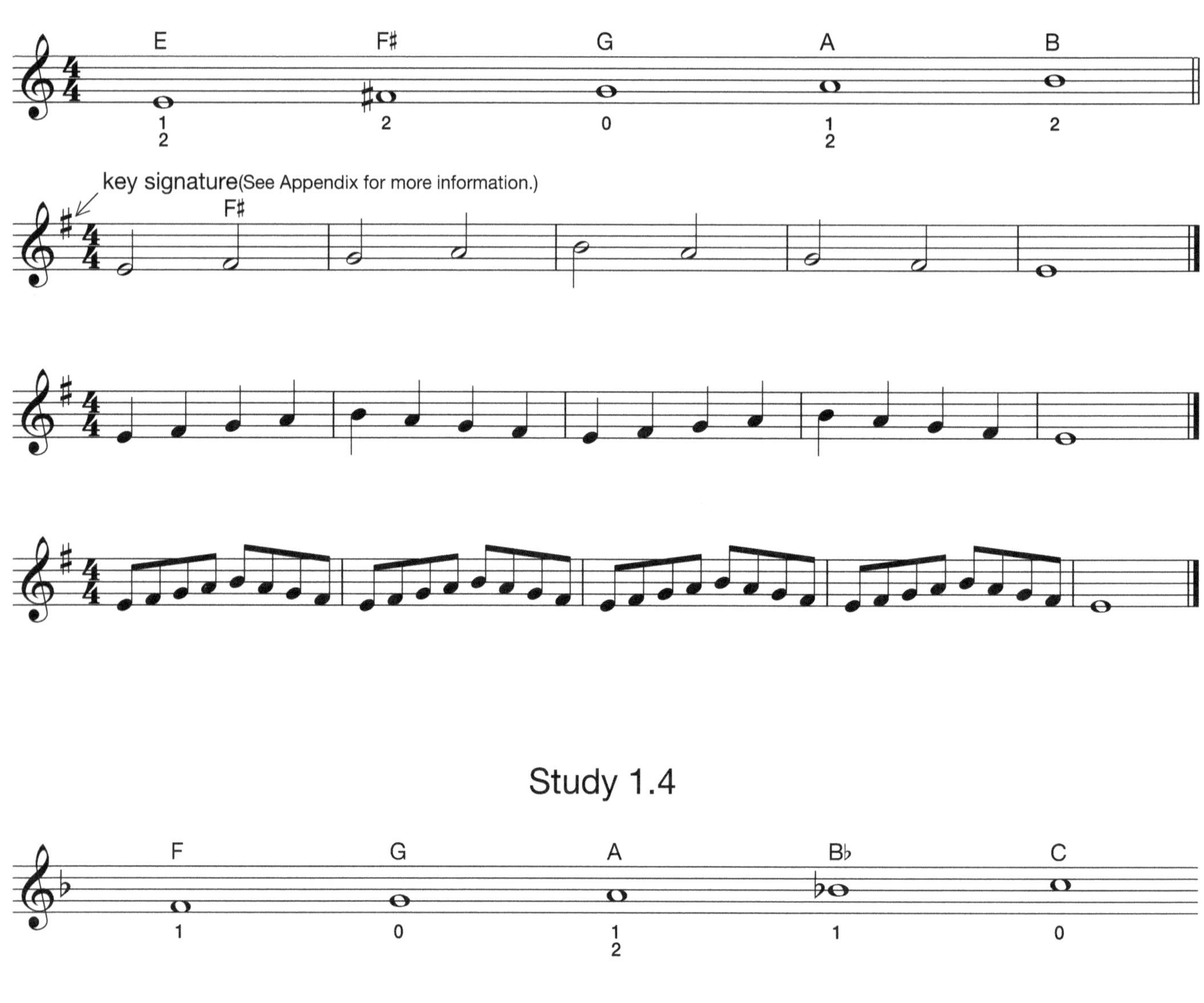

Study 1.4

F G A B♭ C
1 0 1 2 1 0

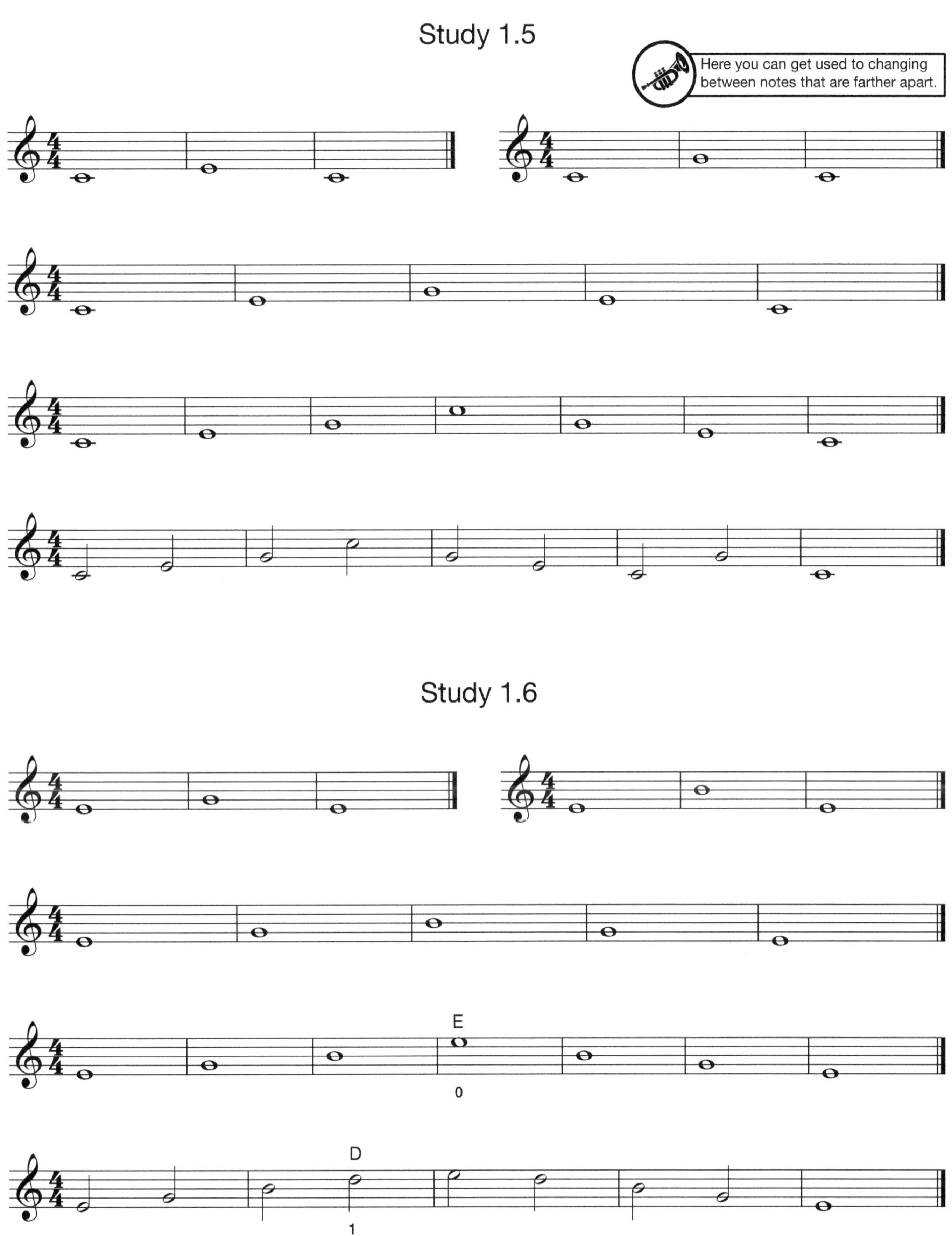
Study 1.5
Here you can get used to changing between notes that are farther apart.
Study 1.6
E
0
D
1

Part 2 - Basic Scales

Study 2.1A

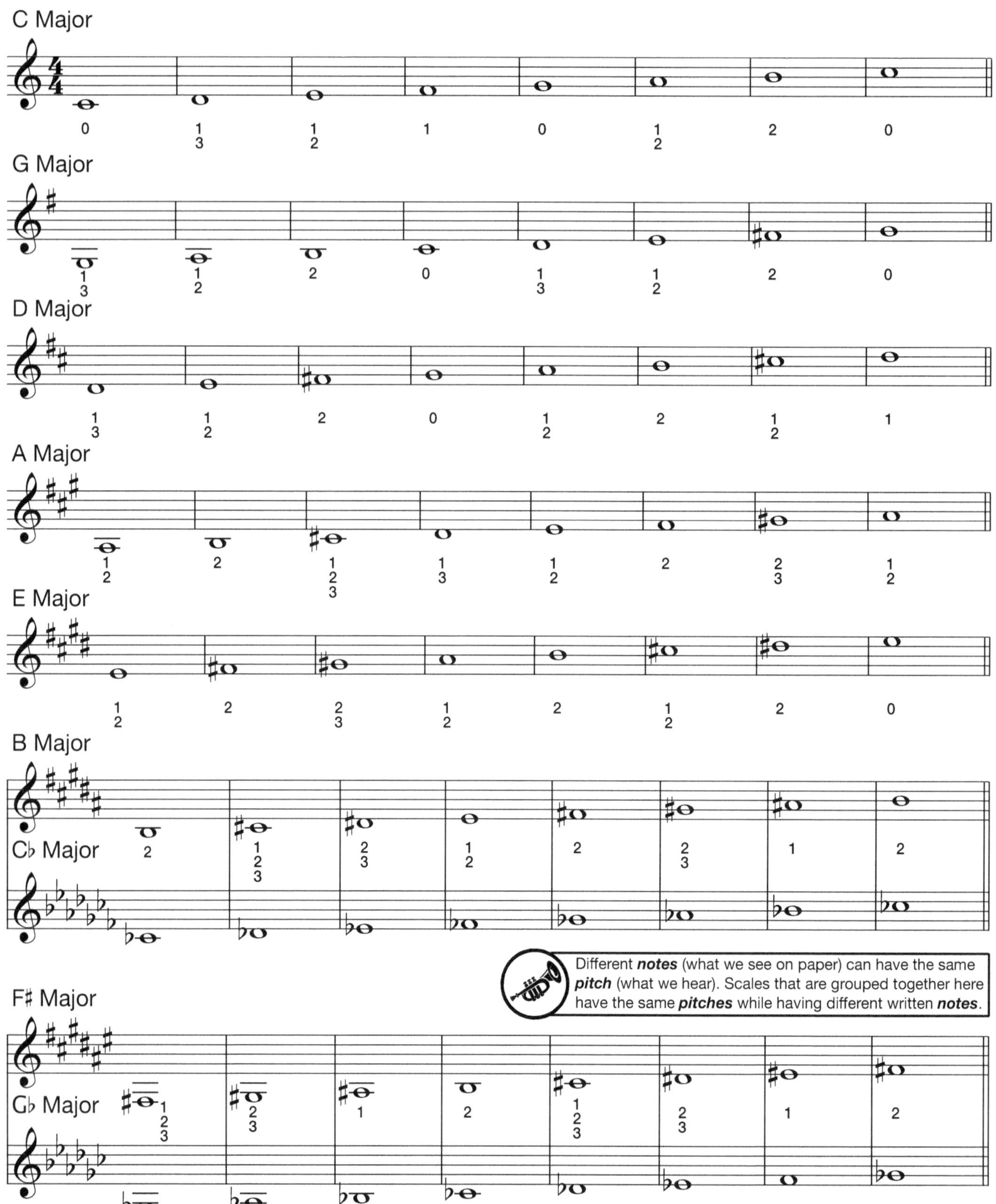

C♯ Major

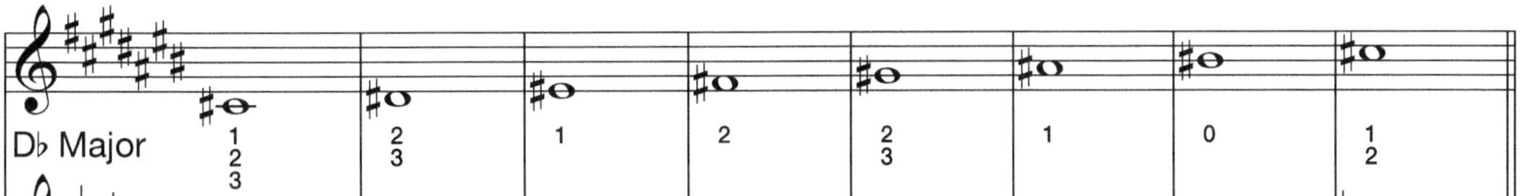

1 2 3 | 2 3 | 1 | 2 | 2 3 | 1 | 0 | 1 2

D♭ Major

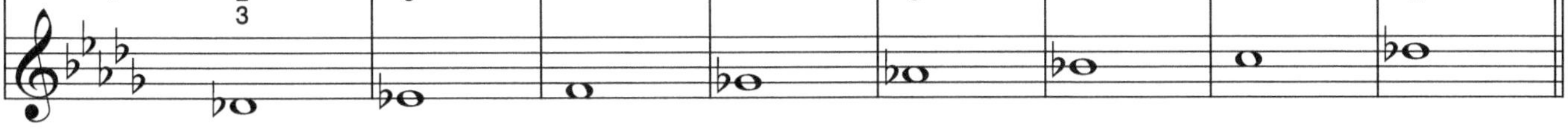

A♭ Major

2 3 | 1 | 0 | 1 2 3 | 2 3 | 1 | 0 | 2 3

E♭ Major

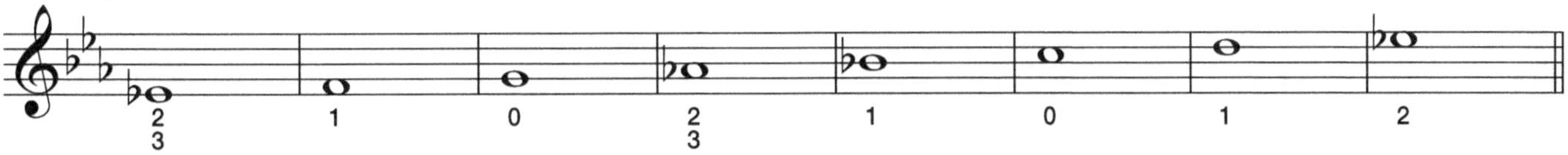

2 3 | 1 | 0 | 2 3 | 1 | 0 | 1 | 2

B♭ Major

1 | 0 | 1 3 | 2 3 | 1 | 0 | 1 2 | 1

F Major

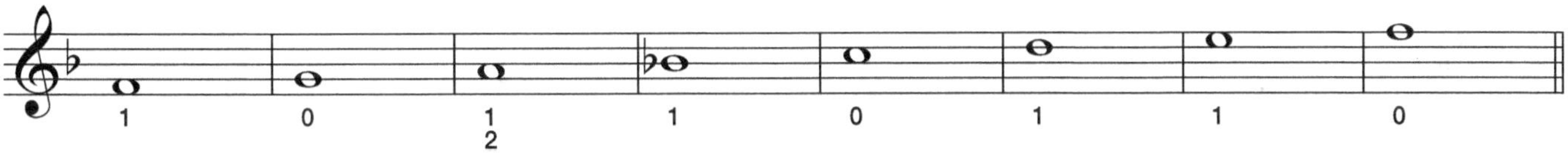

1 | 0 | 1 2 | 1 | 0 | 1 | 1 | 0

C Major

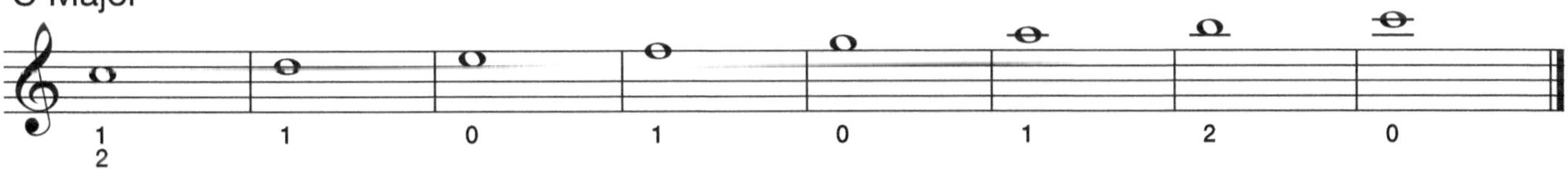

1 2 | 1 | 0 | 1 | 0 | 1 | 2 | 0

More About Fingerings for Low D and Low C♯/D♭

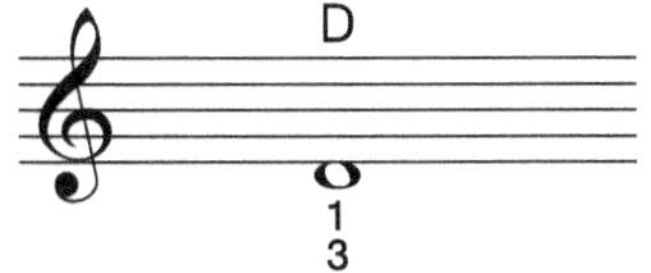

extend the 3rd valve slide a bit

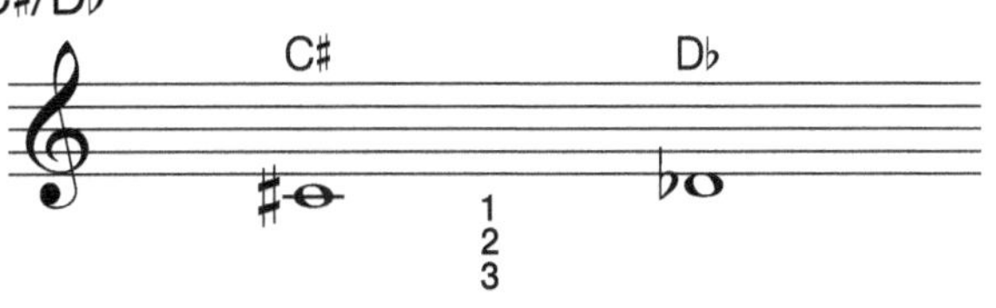

extend the 3rd valve slide a lot

At first, just get used to using the 3rd valve slide while pressing the valves. Then, work with an experienced trumpeter and maybe a tuner to find out the best slide positions for your trumpet to be in tune on these pitches.

Study 2.1B

natural minor

A♯ Minor
B♭ Minor
F Minor
C Minor
G Minor
D Minor
A Minor

Study 2.2A

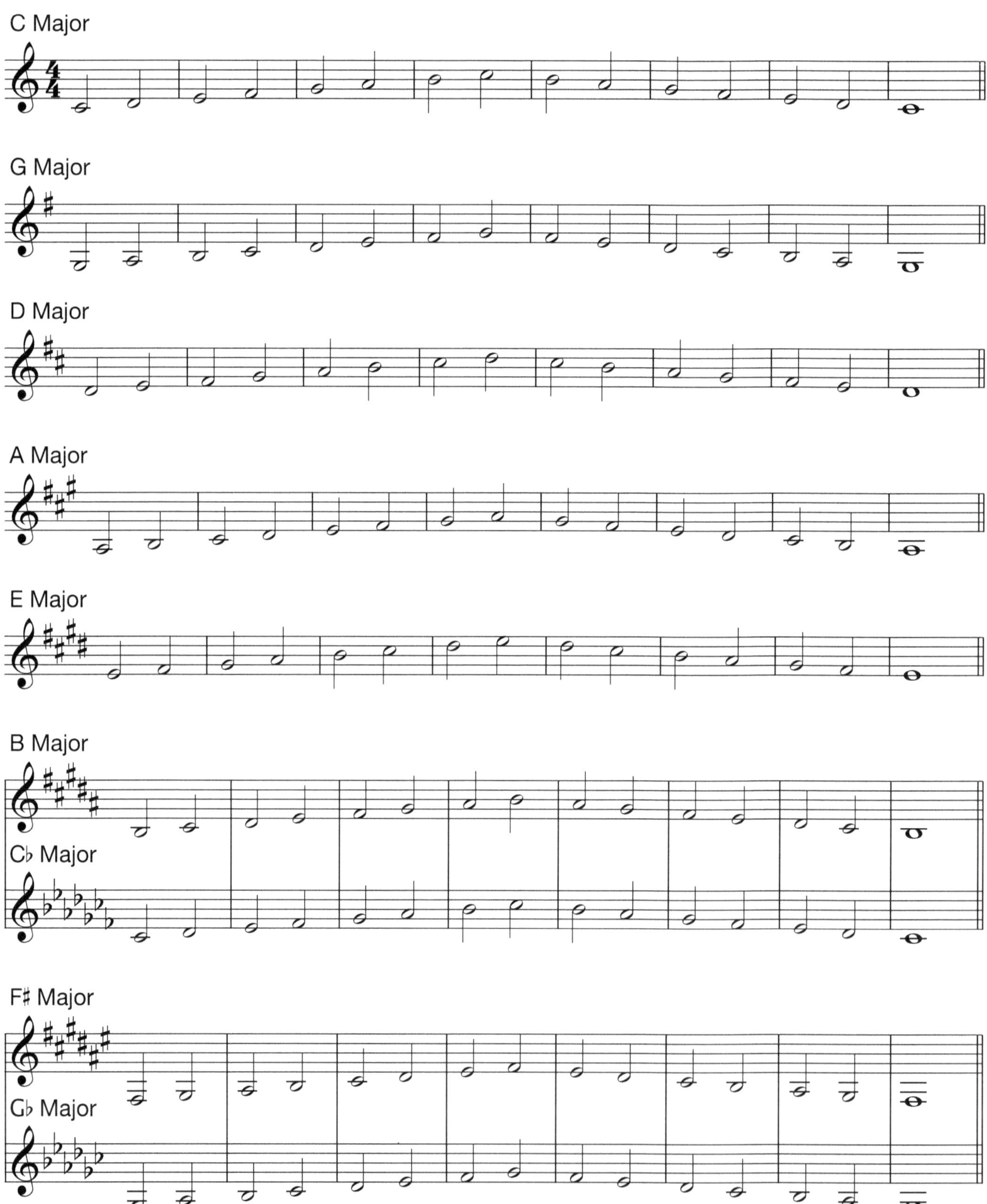

Start with octaves that are comfortable, but work toward playing each scale in multiple octaves.

Study 2.2B
natural minor

A♯ Minor
B♭ Minor
F Minor
C Minor
G Minor
D Minor
A Minor

Study 2.3A

This scale rhythm is is good to know
for school and honor band auditions.
C Major
G Major
D Major
A Major
E Major
B Major
C♭ Major
F♯ Major
G♭ Major

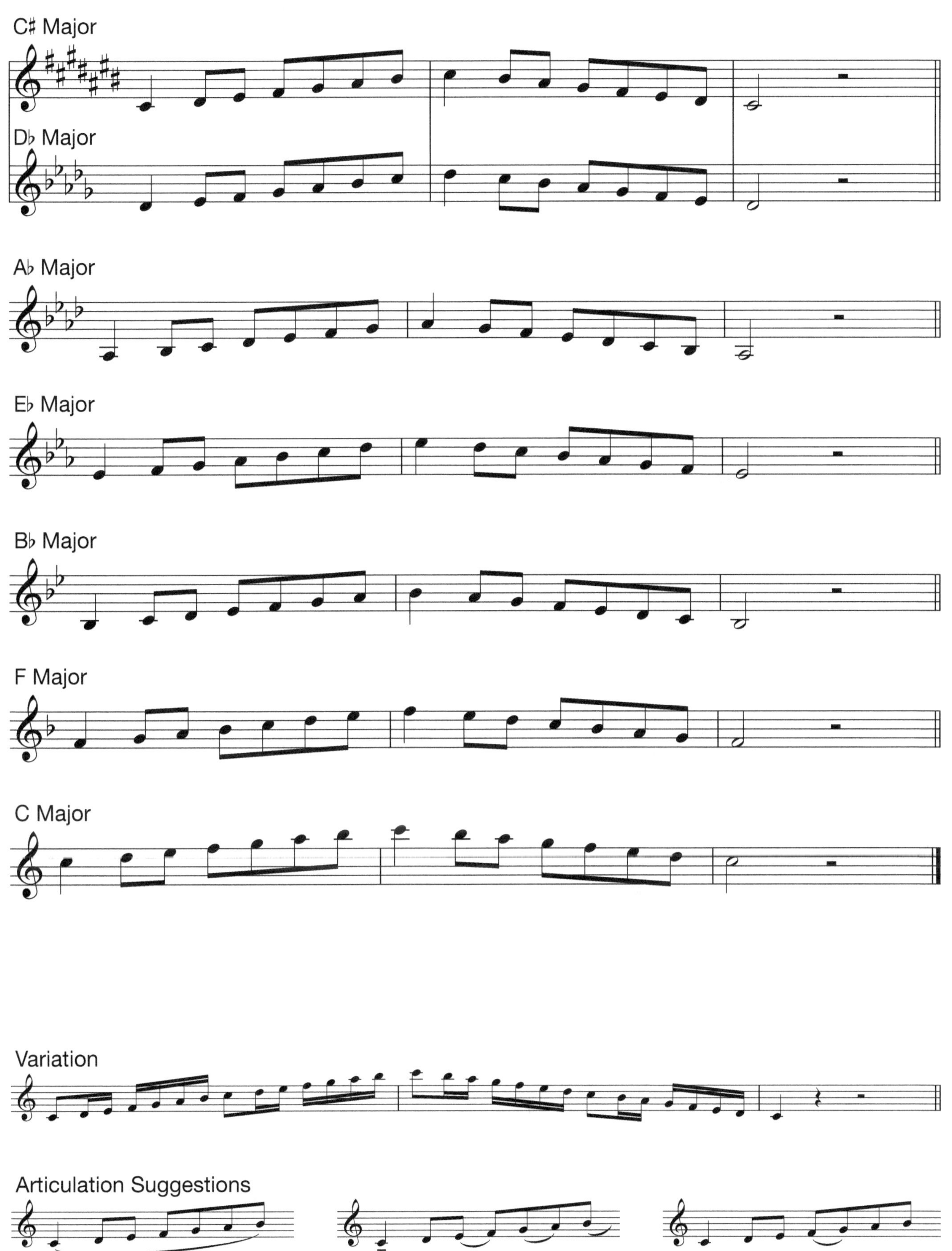
C♯ Major
D♭ Major
A♭ Major
E♭ Major
B♭ Major
F Major
C Major
Variation
Articulation Suggestions

Study 2.3B
melodic minor

A♯ Minor
0
1
2
B♭ Minor
F Minor
C Minor
G Minor
D Minor
A Minor
Variation
Articulation Suggestions

Study 2.4A
scale with the 9th

C♯ Major
D♭ Major
A♭ Major
E♭ Major
B♭ Major
F Major
C Major
Variation
Articulation Suggestions

Study 2.4B
melodic minor

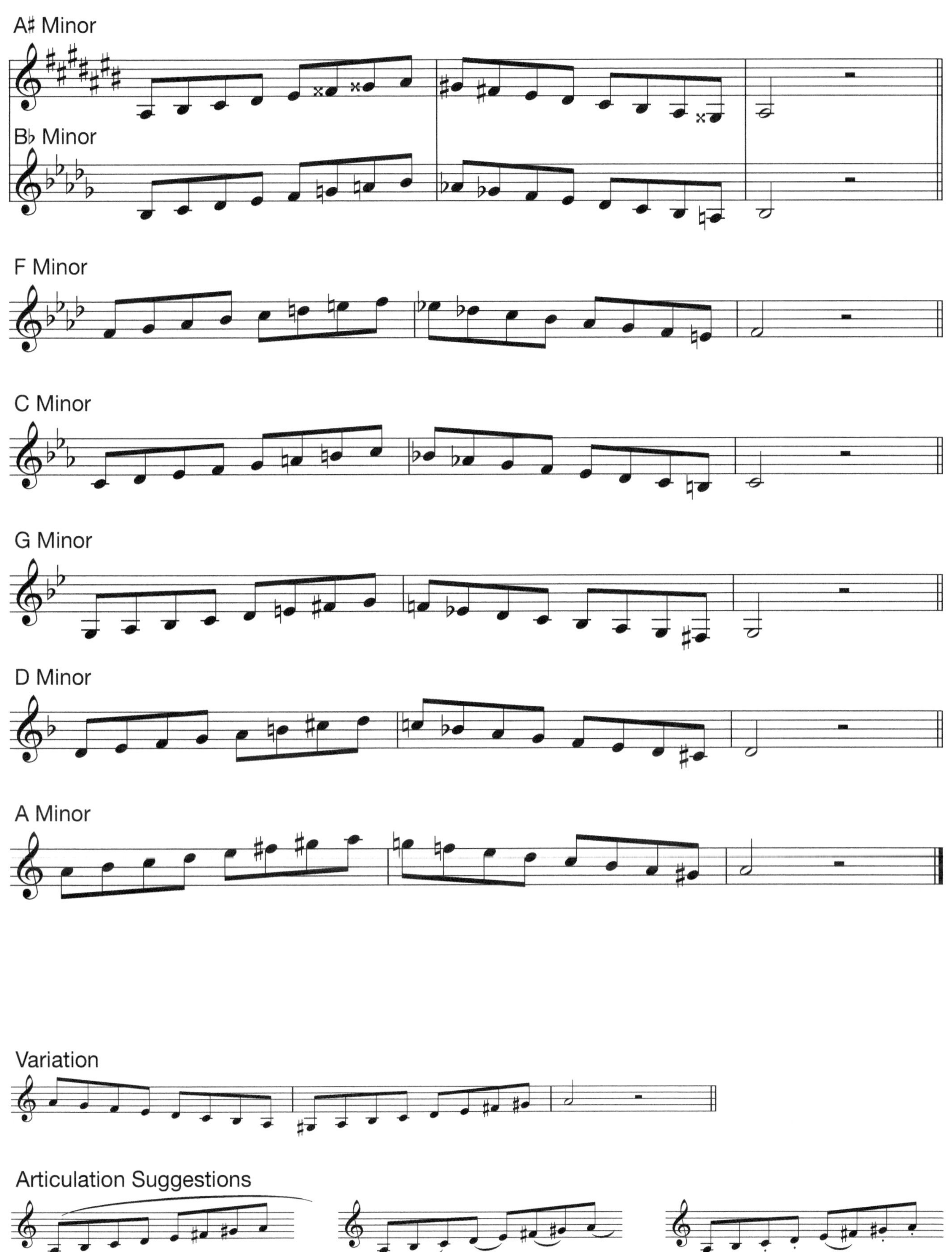
A♯ Minor
B♭ Minor
F Minor
C Minor
G Minor
D Minor
A Minor
Variation
Articulation Suggestions

Part 3 - Basic Arpeggios

Study 3.1A
basic arpeggios

Be careful not to tighten your lips too much on the way up or loosen them too much on the way down. Aim for the best sound on each note.

3.1B
basic arpeggios

A♯ Minor
B♭ Minor
F Minor
C Minor
G Minor
D Minor
A Minor

Study 3.2A

C♯ Major
D♭ Major
A♭ Major
E♭ Major
B♭ Major
F Major
C Major

Study 3.2B

A♯ Minor
B♭ Minor
F Minor
C Minor
G Minor
D Minor
A Minor

Part 4 - Intermediate Scales

Study 4.1A
scale in thirds

C♯ Major
D♭ Major
A♭ Major
E♭ Major
B♭ Major
F Major
C Major
Variation
Articulation Suggestions

Study 4.1B
scale in thirds

(See Appendix for more information on ***thirds***.)

A Minor

E Minor

B Minor

F♯ Minor

C♯ Minor

G♯ Minor

A♭ Minor

D♯ Minor

E♭ Minor

A♯ Minor
B♭ Minor
F Minor
C Minor
G Minor
D Minor
A Minor
Variation
Articulation Suggestions

Study 4.2A
duple to triple

E Major
3
B Major
C♭ Major
F♯ Major
G♭ Major

C♯ Major
D♭ Major
A♭ Major
E♭ Major
B♭ Major

F Major
3
C Major
3
Make sure the three notes of each triplet are evenly spaced over the beat. It's easy to play one note slightly shorter or longer than the other two.
Variations
6
Articulation Suggestions

Study 4.2B
duple to triple

C♯ Minor
G♯ Minor
A♭ Minor
D♯ Minor
E♭ Minor

A♯ Minor
B♭ Minor
F Minor
C Minor
G Minor

D Minor
A Minor

Variations
Articulation Suggestions

Study 4.3A

Articulation Suggestions

Study 4.3B

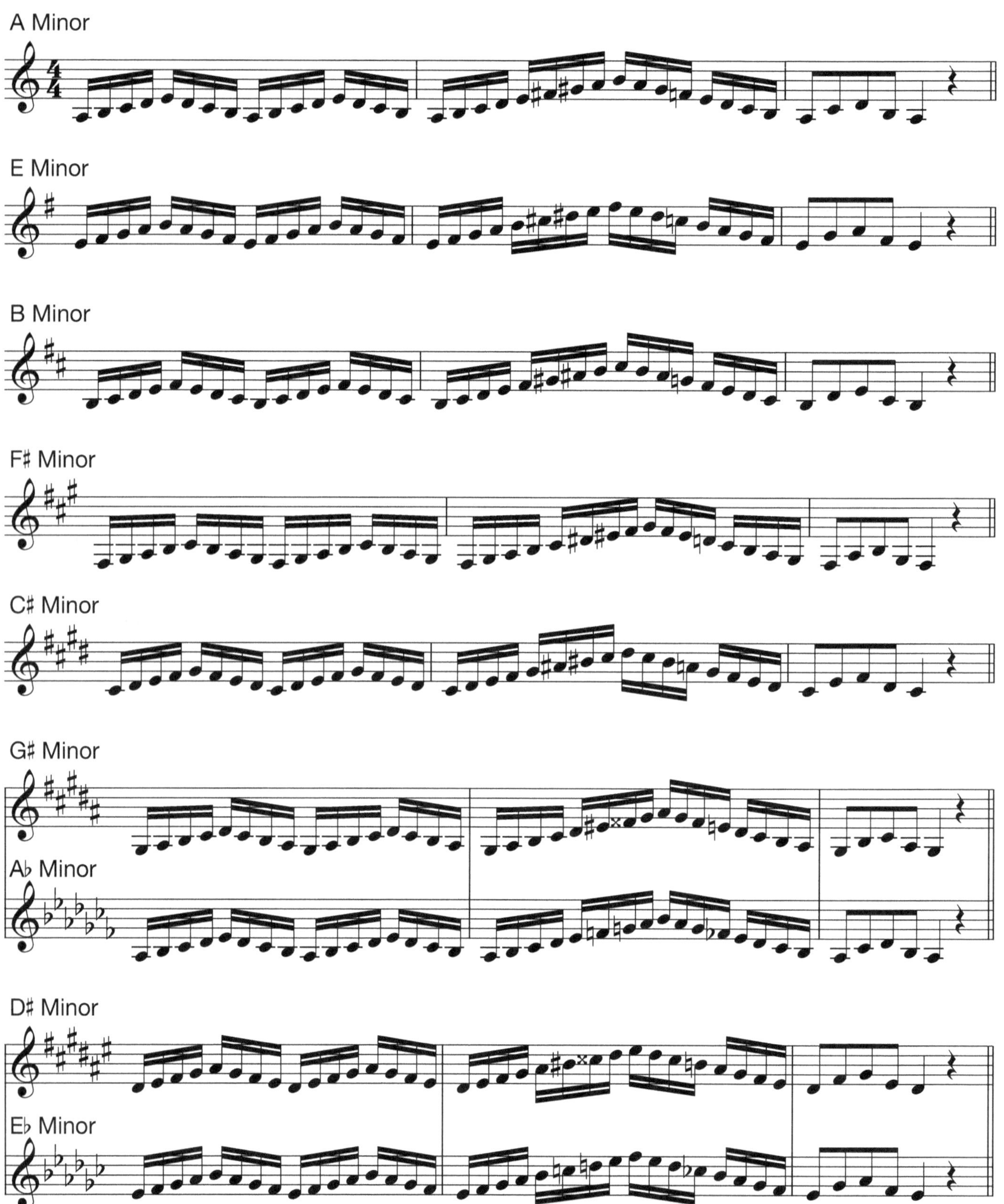

A♯ Minor
B♭ Minor
F Minor
C Minor
G Minor
D Minor
A Minor
Variations
loop and gradually increase tempo
Articulation Suggestions

Study 4.4A

E Major
B Major
C♭ Major
F♯ Major
G♭ Major

C♯ Major
D♭ Major
A♭ Major
E♭ Major
B♭ Major

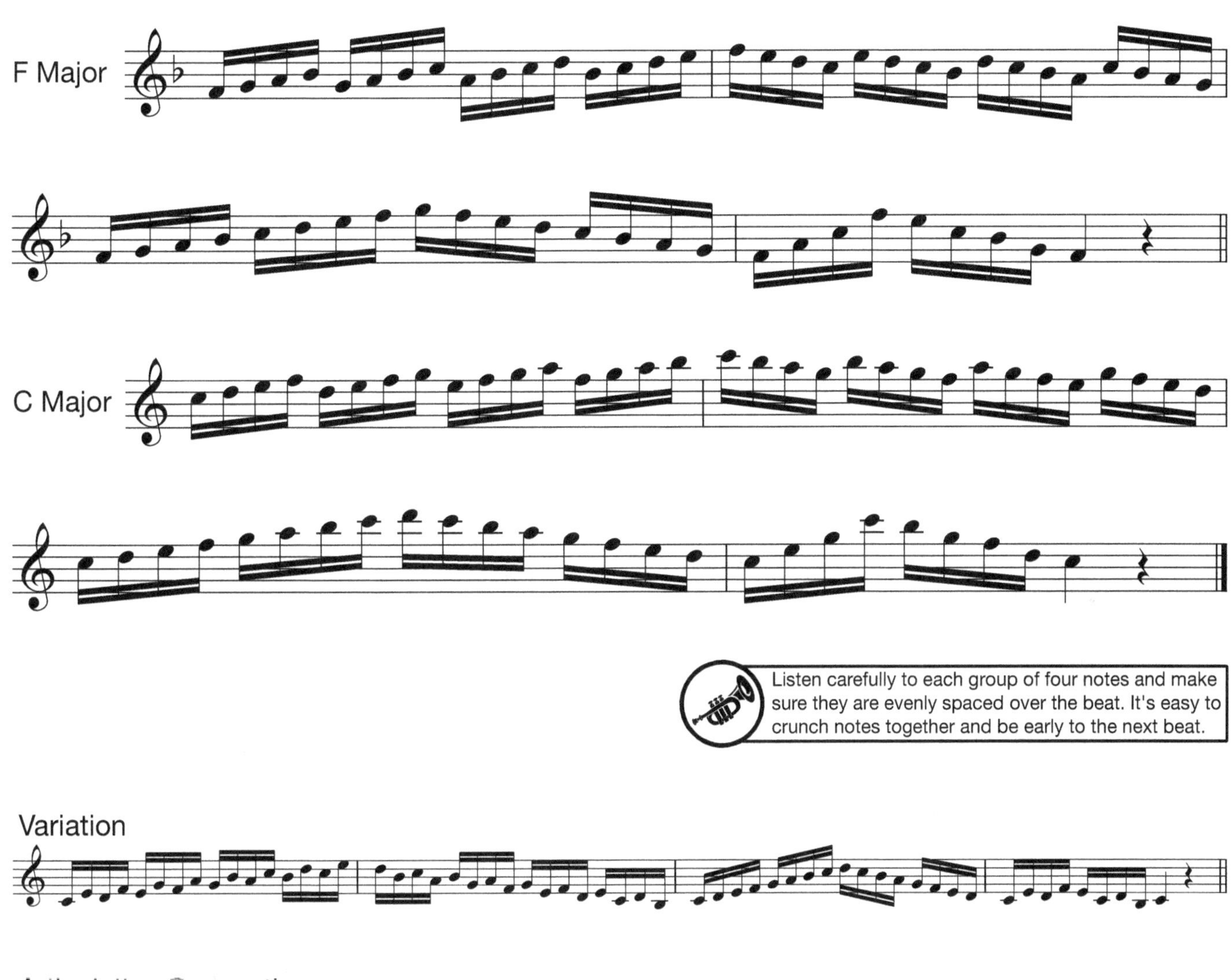

Articulation Suggestions

Study 4.4B

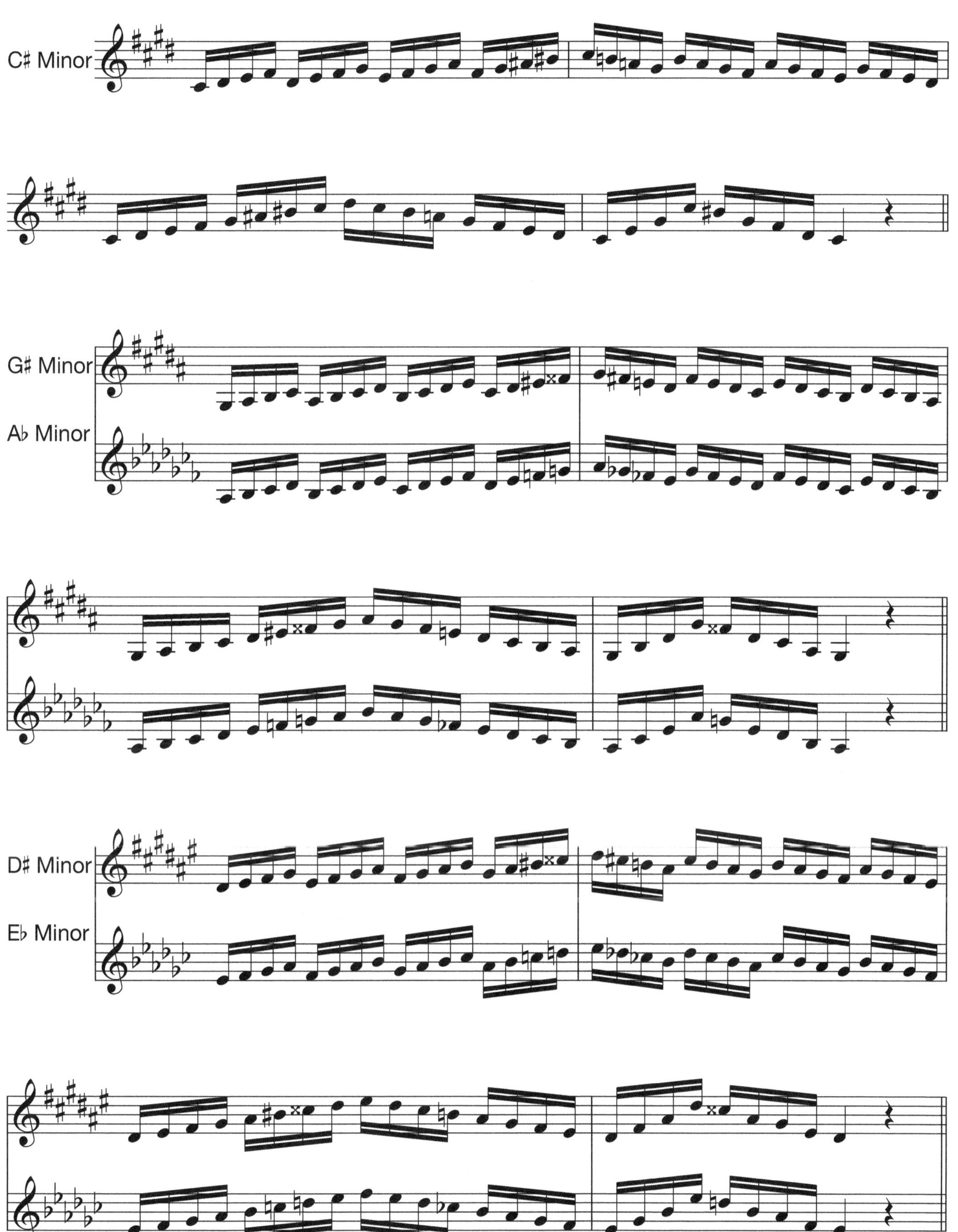
C♯ Minor
G♯ Minor
A♭ Minor
D♯ Minor
E♭ Minor

A♯ Minor
B♭ Minor
F Minor
C Minor
G Minor

D Minor
A Minor

Variation
Articulation Suggestions

Part 5 - Intermediate Arpeggios

Study 5.1A

C♯ Major

D♭ Major

A♭ Major

E♭ Major

B♭ Major

F Major

C Major

Articulation Suggestion

Study 5.1B

A♯ Minor

B♭ Minor

F Minor

C Minor

G Minor

D Minor

A Minor

Articulation Suggestion

Study 5.2A

C♯ Major
D♭ Major
A♭ Major
E♭ Major
B♭ Major
F Major
C Major
Variations

Study 5.2B

A♯ Minor
B♭ Minor
F Minor
C Minor
G Minor
D Minor
A Minor
Variations

Study 5.3A

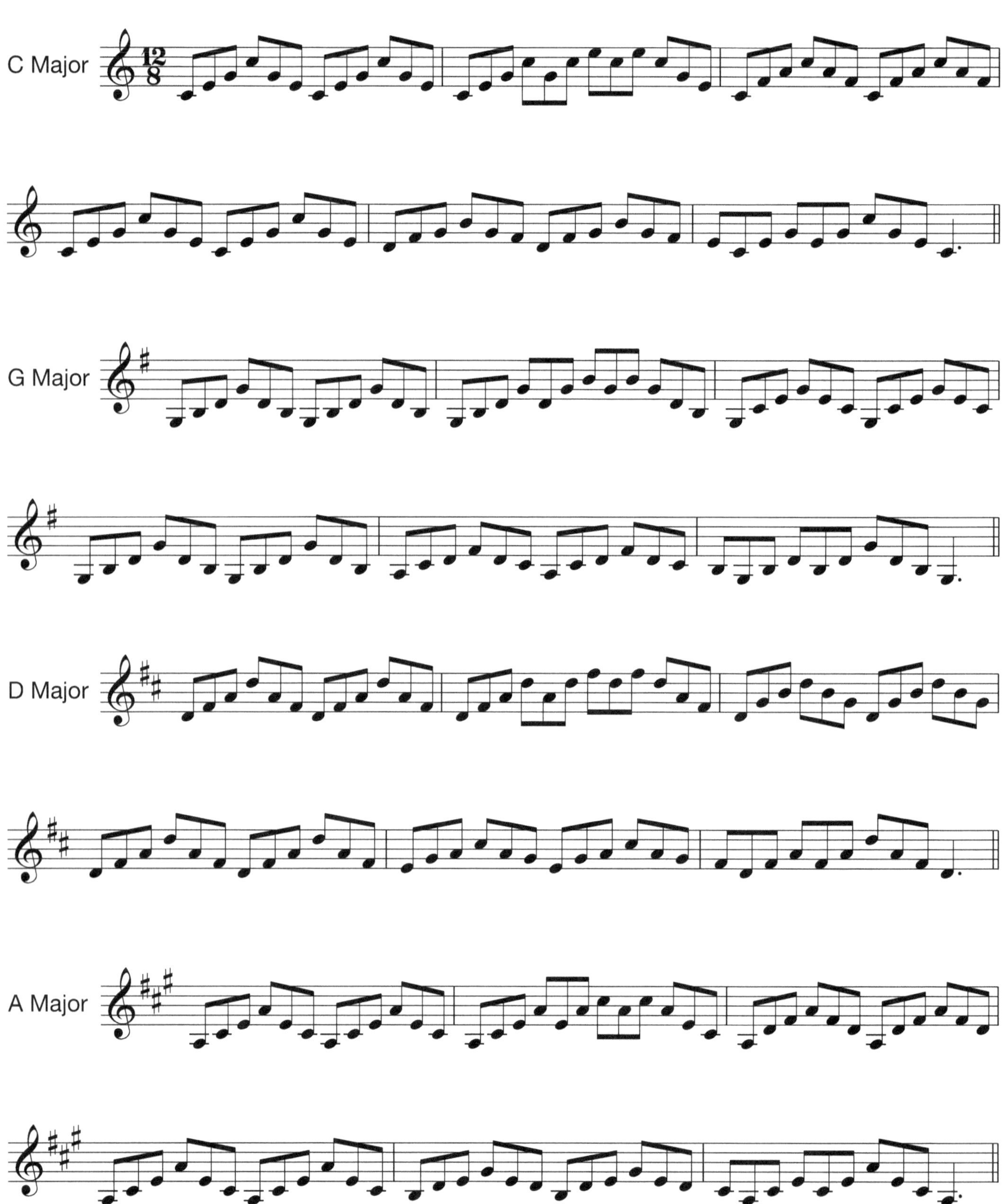

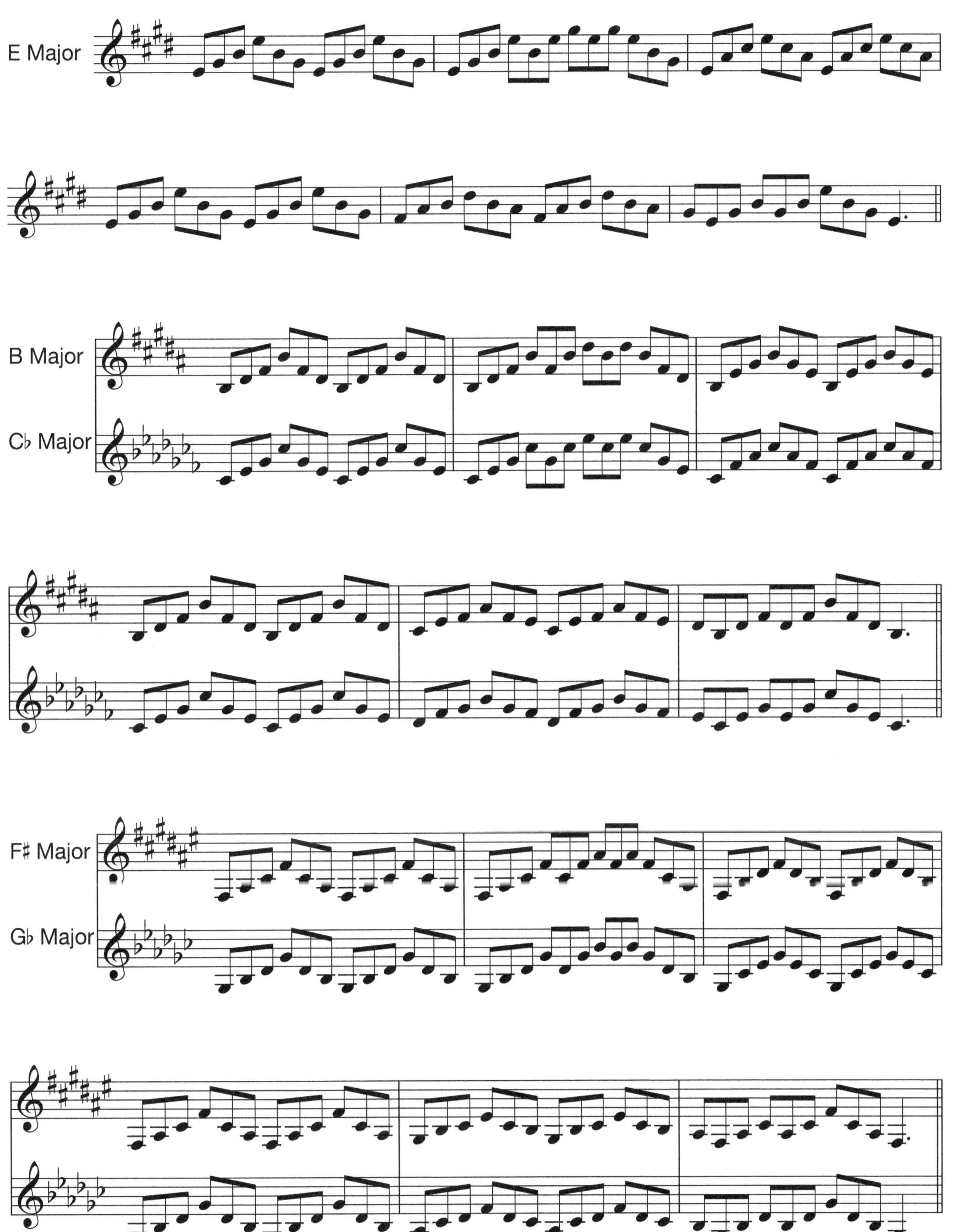
E Major
B Major
C♭ Major
F♯ Major
G♭ Major

C♯ Major
D♭ Major
A♭ Major
E♭ Major
B♭ Major

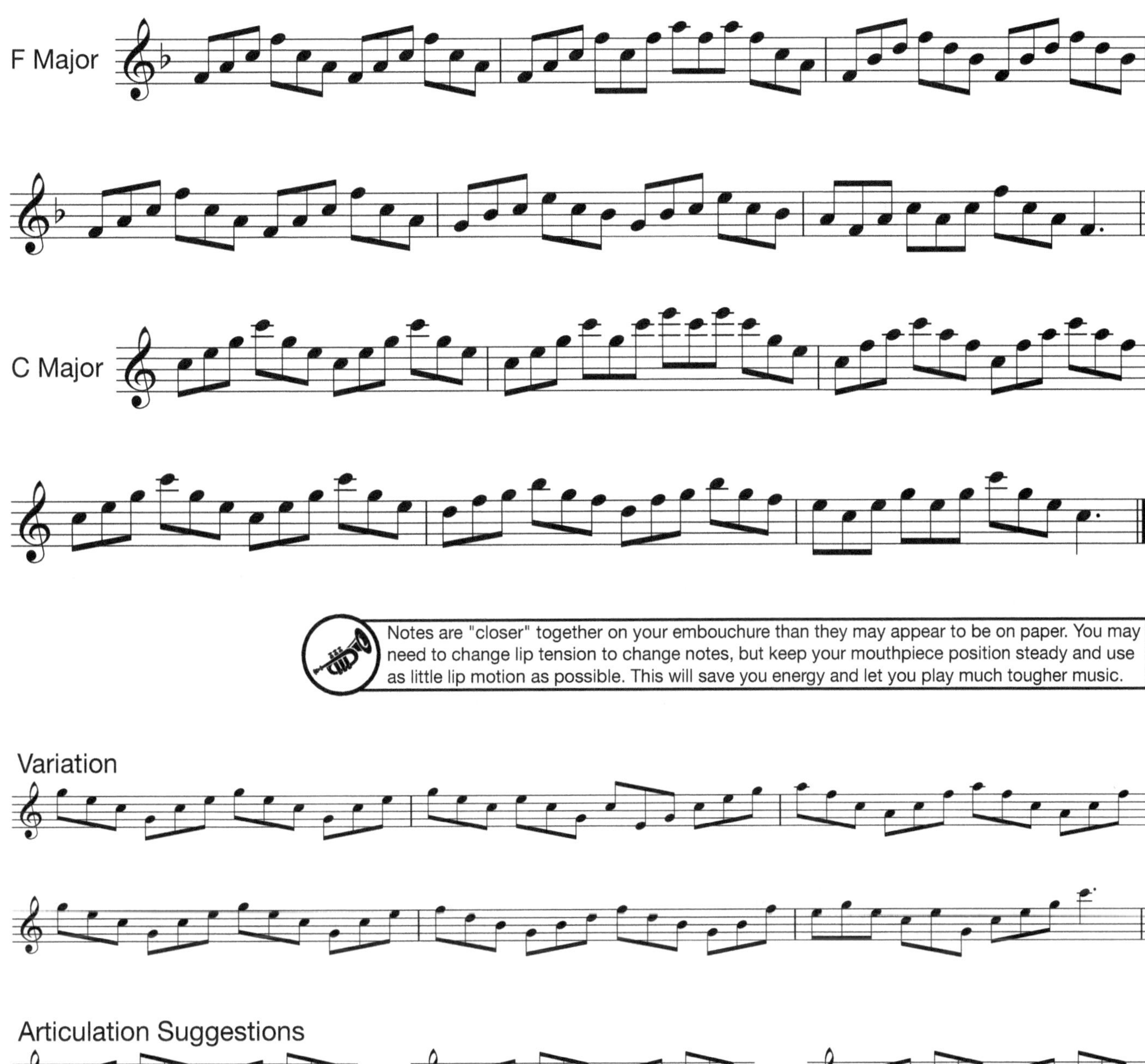
F Major
C Major
Notes are "closer" together on your embouchure than they may appear to be on paper. You may need to change lip tension to change notes, but keep your mouthpiece position steady and use as little lip motion as possible. This will save you energy and let you play much tougher music.
Variation
Articulation Suggestions

Study 5.3B

C♯ Minor
G♯ Minor
A♭ Minor
D♯ Minor
E♭ Minor

A♯ Minor
B♭ Minor
F Minor
C Minor
G Minor

Variation

Articulation Suggestions

Study 5.4A

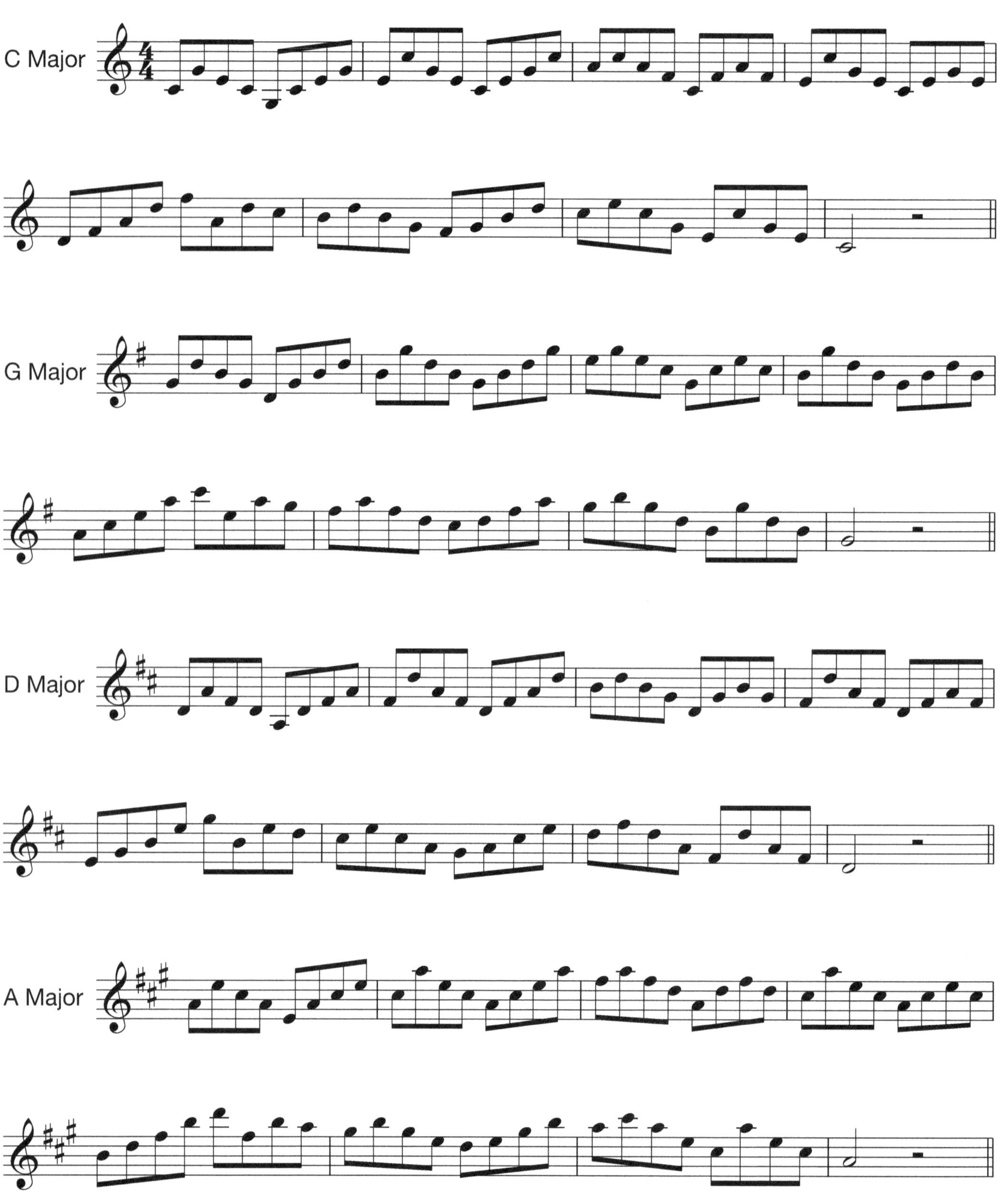

E Major
B Major
C♭ Major
F♯ Major
G♭ Major

C♯ Major
D♭ Major
A♭ Major
E♭ Major
B♭ Major

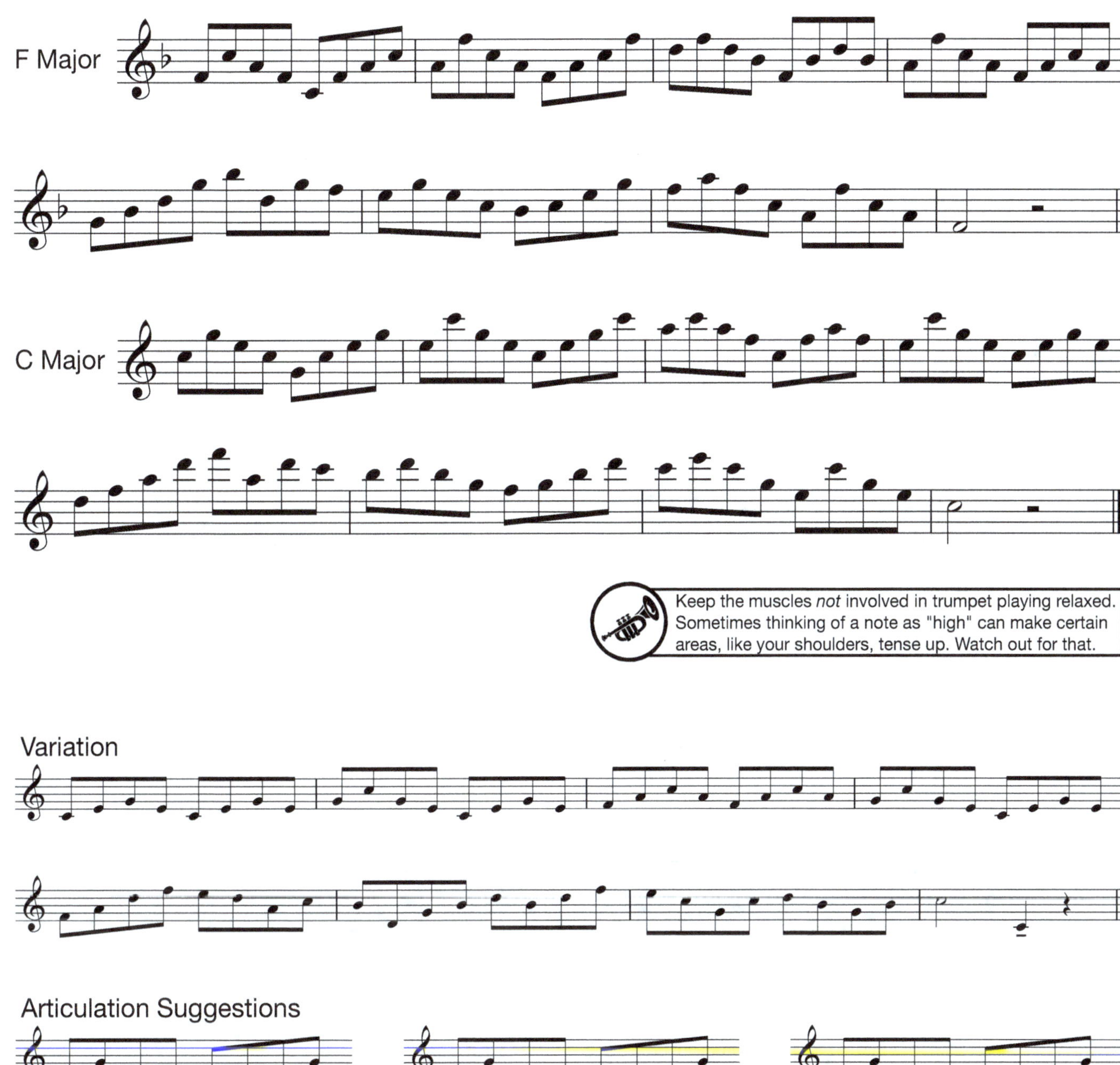
F Major
C Major
Keep the muscles *not* involved in trumpet playing relaxed. Sometimes thinking of a note as "high" can make certain areas, like your shoulders, tense up. Watch out for that.
Variation
Articulation Suggestions

Study 5.4B

C♯ Minor
G♯ Minor
A♭ Minor
D♯ Minor
E♭ Minor

A♯ Minor
B♭ Minor
F Minor
C Minor
G Minor

D Minor
A Minor

Variation
Articulation Suggestions

Part 6 - Extended Studies

Study 6.1

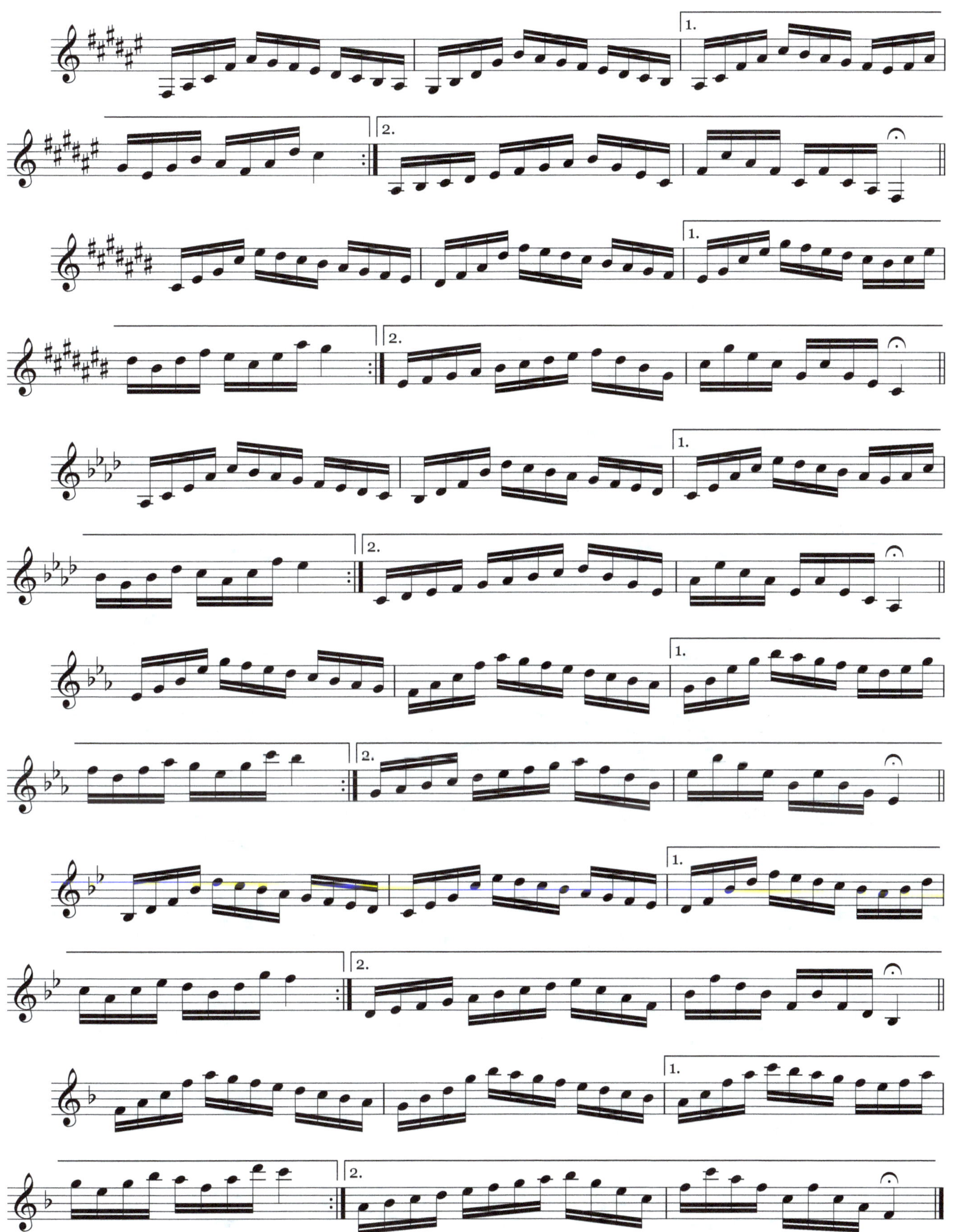
1.
2.
1.
2.
1.
2.
1.
2.
1.
2.
1.
2.

Study 6.2

Study 6.3a

Study 6.3b

Study 6.4

tr
tr
tr
tr
tr
tr

Study 6.5a

Study 6.5b

"14"

Here is the same exercise *ascending* chromatically.

etc. →

Appendix

Scale Degrees and Intervals

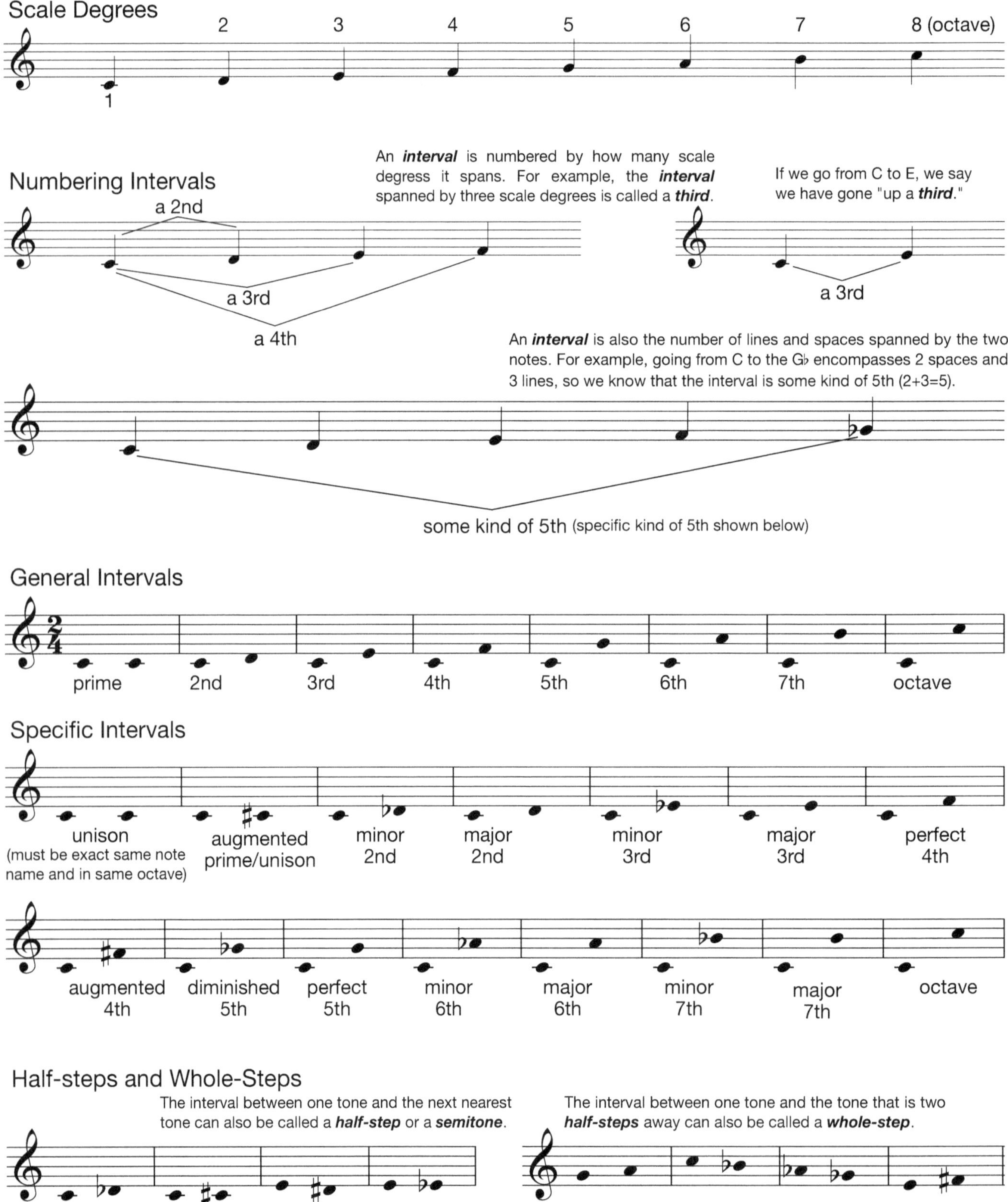

Relatives

Each ***key signature*** is shared by one major and one minor key, and the two are said to be ***relative***. For example, C major is the ***relative major*** of A minor, and A minor is the ***relative minor*** of C major.

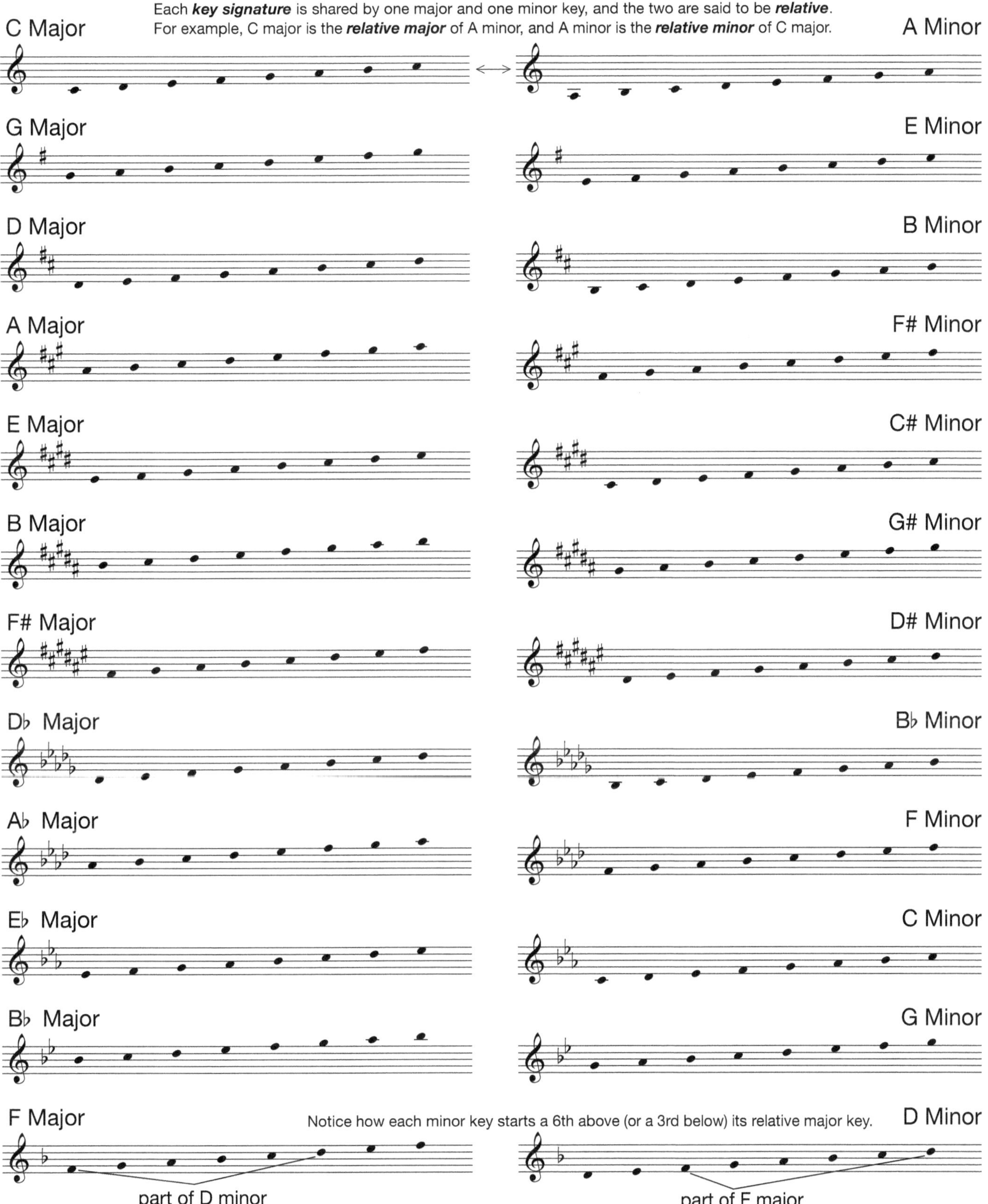

Notice how each minor key starts a 6th above (or a 3rd below) its relative major key.

Parallels

Keys with the same letter name are said to be ***parallel***. For example, C major is the ***parallel major*** of C minor, and C minor is the ***parallel minor*** of C major.
C Major
C Minor
The differences between the major and minor scales are the 3rd, 6th, and 7th scale degrees.
G Major
G Minor
D Major
D Minor
A Major
A Minor
E Major
E Minor
B Major
B Minor
F# Major
F# Minor
C♯ Major
C# Minor
A♭ Major
A♭ Minor
E♭ Major
E♭ Minor
B♭ Major
B♭ Minor
F Major
F Minor

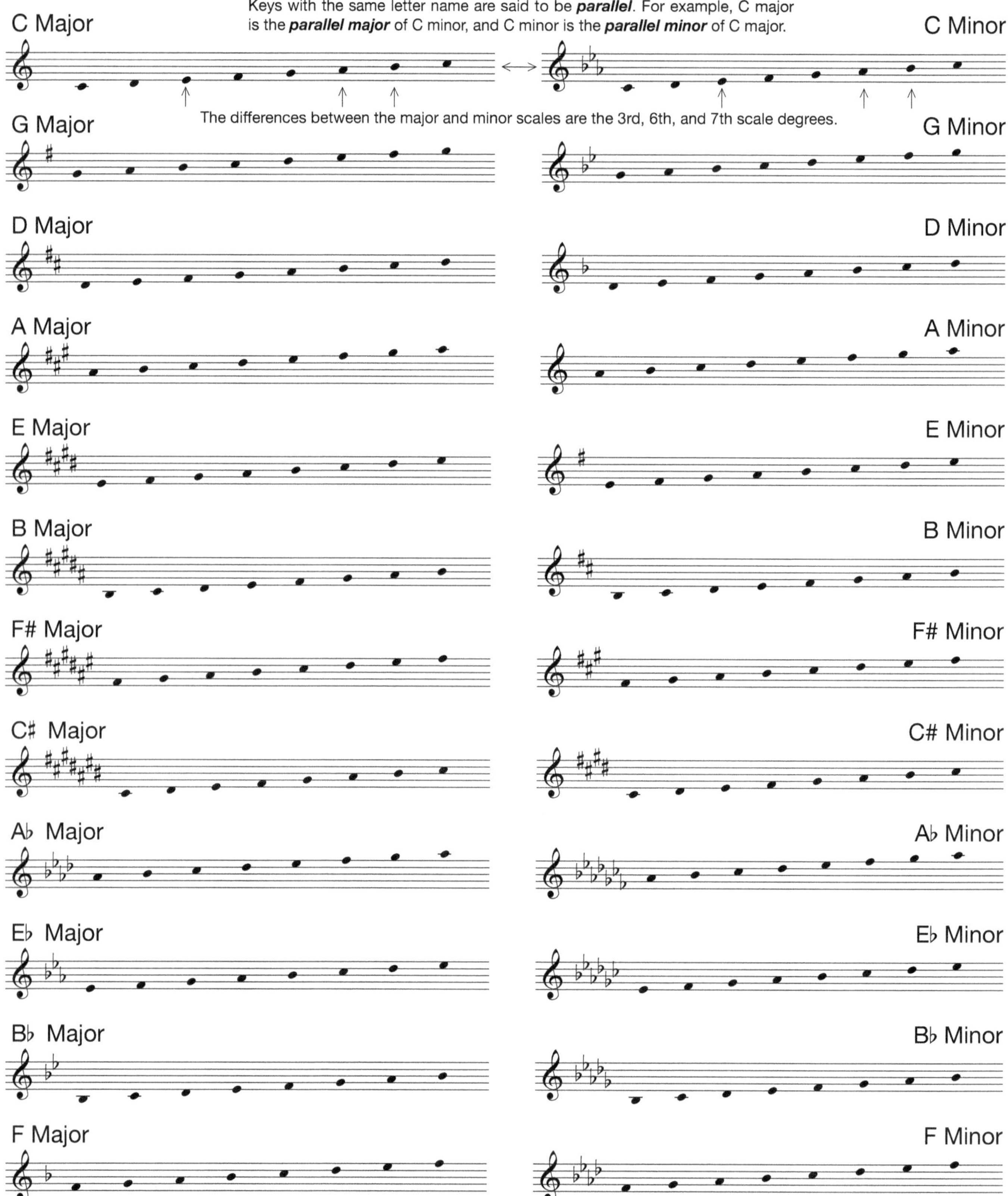

Other Scales

Chromatic Scale

A ***chromatic scale*** is a scale that moves by ***half-steps***, sort of like pressing every key in order on a piano.

Whole-Tone Scale

A ***whole-tone scale*** is a scale that moves by ***whole-steps.*** The terms ***whole-tone*** and ***whole-step*** are used interchangeably.

Scale Ideas for Practicing Chromatic and Whole-Tone Scales

Glossary

accidental — a note that is not part of the scale or key indicated by the key signature; a symbol marking such a note - ♮, ♯, ♭, 𝄪, or 𝄫

chromatic — changing notes by half-steps or semitones; including notes that are not in the key signature

diatonic — only having notes that are in the key signature

enharmonic — a note that has the same pitch as another note but is named differently (e.g. A♯ and B♭)

embouchure — the shape and position of the lips while playing a wind instrument such as the trumpet

half-step — the interval between a pitch and the nearest possible pitch, above or below (e.g. C to the nearest C#, or D to the nearest Db); also known as a semitone

interval — the pitch distance between two notes; the number of letter names the distance spans (e.g. A to the E above is a fifth, spanning the five notes A, B, C, D, and E)

key signature — the part of the music staff that tells you which notes have sharps or flats

key — a phrase (e.g. "G major") naming the tonic and scale that has the notes the music will mostly use; (e.g. A simple piece in G major might use G, A, B, C, D, E, and F♯, and end on a G.)

measure — a unit of music between two vertical "bar lines"; also called a bar

note — a symbol indicating a tone to be played, how long you hold it, and a name for the tone made up of a letter, A through G, either by itself or with an accidental - ♮, ♯, ♭, 𝄪, or 𝄫

octave — the interval that spans a note and the next nearest note with the *exact* same name

parallel — having the same tonic note but in a different mode (e.g. C major and C minor are parallels)

pitch — the actual sound of a note (B and C♭ are the same pitch, but not the same note.)

relative — having the same key signature but a different tonic (e.g. C major and A minor are relatives)

scale degree — a note's position in a scale, starting with the tonic as scale degree 1

tempo — the pace of the music, described by a word or phrase or by a number showing how many beats there are per minute

time signature — a symbol telling you how many beats are in each measure and what note value is counted as a beat (e.g. "3/4" means three beats per measure and the quarter-note gets one beat)

tonic — the focus or main note of a key or scale; also called the key-note; the music will seem to "pull toward" this note and sound complete when ending on it (e.g. The tonic of C major is C.)

whole-step — an interval made up of two half-steps or semitones (e.g. from C up to the nearest D, or from F down to the nearest E♭); also called a whole-tone

Final Suggestions

- You might try playing a major scale and then immediately playing its relative minor scale. For example, play C major on page 4 followed by A minor on page 40. Then G major followed by E minor, and so on. This could help reinforce your understanding of how major and minor keys share key signatures and relate to each other.

- Once you're comfortable with each scale in a study, play the entire study as one exercise. For example, on Study 2.3, start with the C Major scale and play through each double-bar line, keeping steady tempo, until you reach the final bar line on the next page.

- After learning a scale in a comfortable octave, play the same scale in a different octave. Playing scales can be useful for extending your comfortable range, both high and low.

- If you're a beginner, use the simpler scales and arpeggios, especially those in Part 1, to develop a solid sound and embouchure. Sound and embouchure issues are difficult things to fix later on.

- Always change notes with as little change in your lips as possible. Notes may *look* far apart on printed music, but this does not mean that they are far apart on your embouchure or that an interval requires a large shift in lip tension.

- For each scale, pick a tempo that allows you to play every note and rhythm accurately while keeping the tempo steady. Then, gradually increase the tempo from there.

- Use a metronome when you practice. Even though a lot of the music you play will not have strict tempo, you want to be able to have as much control of your rhythm and timing as possible. You want any tempo fluctuations to be *your* tempo fluctuations, and not just random results of poor technique. Metronome work can give you that control.

- Record yourself. This will let you hear some aspects of your playing you might not notice while you are playing, such as unwanted tempo fluctations or a note that doesn't sound quite as nice the others you played.

- Use a mirror. While it might not be worthwhile to obsess over having a perfect embouchure, periodically watching yourself play in a mirror can help you catch some bad habits, such as unnecessarily tilting the instrument or playing with it pointing off at a significant angle.

- Use a tuner and a pitch source. A tuner is good for pointing out which tones you tend to play sharp or flat, and can also show you any tones that you may have "gotten used to" playing out of tune and which now sound in tune to you. A pitch source, such as any device playing a sustained drone, can be useful for you to hear how your trumpet playing mixes with other musical sounds around you.

- Rest whenever you need to. It's important to "push it" sometimes and build endurance, but if you find yourself forcing something or muscling something because you are tired, then it's time to rest. Forceful playing will not be how you ultimately want to play, so there's no reason to risk that becoming a habit.

- Don't force anything. Trumpet playing is much more about accuracy, finesse, and finding the "sweet spot" of every note than it is about strength. Even though some strengthening is required to play the trumpet, sheer muscle power rarely works.

Additional Information

Please visit ***www.takecenterstage.today*** for more information on supplemental materials, upcoming books and latest editions. If you have any questions or comments about this book or another of ours, feel free to e-mail us at *info@takecenterstage.today.*

www.ingramcontent.com/pod-product-compliance
Lightning Source LLC
LaVergne TN
LVHW061251100826
845148LV00008B/1096
* 9 7 8 1 7 3 6 0 8 7 6 1 9 *